GREAT
TIMES

GREAT TIMES

BIOGRAPHICAL, LOVE AND GENERAL PHILOSOPHIC LEARNING

MAGNUS KING

GREAT TIMES
BIOGRAPHICAL, LOVE AND GENERAL PHILOSOPHIC LEARNING

iUniverse books may be ordered through booksellers or by contacting:

iUniverse
1663 Liberty Drive
Bloomington, IN 47403
www.iuniverse.com
1-800-Authors (1-800-288-4677)

ISBN: 978-1-5320-1604-2 (sc)
ISBN: 978-1-5320-1605-9 (e)

Print information available on the last page.

iUniverse rev. date: 02/07/2017

(1)　THESE DIRTY PAGES OF WAR

These dirty pages of war
Compels our pace
In the midst of grace
From above; so shallow
Its ticktock scenes
And so long—
So long beneath our fathers refuge camp

And this god of hunger
Curses our years
Blinding our eyes with crimson tears
Without desire we bear a cross
Suffer a loss
And lay in sack-clothing
For supplication; for peace
In this millennium
And that this dirty war may die

Author's Notes

God save the Niger Area

(2)   REVENGE IS NO SEASON IN HELL

Revenge is no season in hell
For there's no unbeliever there
   They all sing and praise
   They do shout and hail
   The King of Glory

The gates never close to open
The sealed doors, not next to broken
   The streets, ever dark
   Windows ever mark
   The men of folly

It's never the Son of their vows
Nesting beneath the Hades South
   Where no rain nor cool
   Neither fist nor duel
   O LORD Almighty!

AUTHOURS'S NOTES: aabbc, ddeec, ffggc

In each stanza, the first two lines has the same syllable count. Likewise the last three lines in each stanza. More like "8-8-5-5-5, 8-8-5-5-5, 8-8-5-5-5"

Truly, there's no unbeliever in hell
Luke 16:19-31

It's not the Son of their vows nesting beneath Hades south: it's not their wish to be in hell.
"No rain nor cool, no fist nor duel": there's no rage nor quarrels of some kind nor fighting in hell.
All praise God and further intercede on behalf of those who are not yet dead to perhaps see if that might save they themselves.

So, who ever said "Revenge is a season in hell"?

(3)   A KNIGHT MEETS THE QUEEN OF ASIA

Knight: Hello! My Lady

Queen: Hi! Sir King

Knight: Now, permit this Knight to ask one thing of you.
    Permit this Knight to ask a question of fate

Queen: OK

Knight: No my Lady. You should say "Granted"
    Or proceed with courage and fill my ears with delight

Queen: Very well Sir King....Granted.

Knight: Has my Lady a king?
    Or has another noble man fixed the sun on her fourth finger?

(No response)

Knight: My Lady is but silent, I wonder why?

Queen: Happy New Year....My fingers are jeweled.

Knight: It's but a question
    My Lady has broken the code of conversation

Queen: Gratitude

Knight: My lips has not betrayed my meaning

Queen: Refrain. Goodnight.

Knight: Funny to the very heights. It's but noon here in the pistol land
    The sun is yet to bring us to the revolution
    But if that be your last words...I accept.

Queen: Very well
    Goodnight.

Knight: Goodnight sounds more displeasing
    My Lady, my true name is trigger in combat and Barnabas at war.

(Another silence)

Knight: Do not think of me as a man of laurels
    For I am clothed still in shining armour.

Queen: What then do you seek from me?
    For a knight is unworthy of my fourth finger

Knight:.....Smiling....
    Truly, my Lady is prettier than the moon
    And brighter than the sun.
    But her dark complexion tells me she's still of this earth.

Queen: I am a goddess of beauty....It's not pride.
    It's my nature.
    Now, tell me, of what kingdom do you hail from?
    And of what adventures have you accomplished to gain my attention?

Knight: My garment is made of cloud
    And my sword sheathed with honour
    I have sailed the seven seas
    My people love me for I have shielded them
    And set free many children.
    My scars are made from battles
    And shadows of warfare.
    Although I am from the pistol land
    I still know of treasures with milk and honey.

(She sighed, but silence continued)

Knight: Look at your eyes....I have seen them in dreams
    Dreams and visions that Angels spoke only to me about
    Even when you cry they still look like shining stars from the sky

(she laughed)

Queen: Sir King your tongue betrays your meaning. You lie!

Knight: No my lady, I could never lie to a beautiful woman
        It's a crime against nature
        Heaven will never forgive me

(She smiled and laughed out loud)

Knight: Tell me your dreams and I'll bring it to life
        kiss me now, and I'll meet you at the foot of the aisle
        My sword, your crown, forever in a sunny town.

She reached for me, as I her.
As she was about to...,my alarm rang....I woke up. And behold it was a dream.
I tried getting back to sleep but I couldn't

AUTHOR'S NOTES:

Pistol land: Africa(The shape of Africa looks like a pistol)
Scars of battles and shadows of warfare: Are the injuries and honour sustained from battles and wars.
I have sailed the seven seas: I have traveled to many countries.
My garment is made of cloud: Theocratic in nature

Am still clothed in shining armour: I am not of little value
Trigger in combat: Nigeria is the trigger of Africa's pistol shape
Barnabas in war: Fearless

Sun on the fourth finger: Wedding or engagement ring...Are you married?

(4)　THE BONDS OF BROTHERHOOD

The bonds of brotherhood!!!
Has always run deep within these walls
The slandering of beauty is not heard
Nor was there any whisper of poison
Like the dew of Hermon
Falling on Mount Zion
Where two or more are gathered in His Name
That circle of prayer
And the everlasting chain of faith
Binding them together, forever
In the sweet melody of righteousness
And harmony of peace.

That is the future
Where was the past?

In the garden of Eden
Where the serpent bites
Charming loyalty to disobedience
Where two which is one
And man was sent from fortitude
Because of misdeed and attitude
Betraying the bond between man and God
That was division

This is the present
The music of nightfall
Is playing through my ears
I look but see only shadows
And monsters from the pit
Of hell coming forth
From the very depth of nightfall
They surround me like a traffic of demons
Now, I long for the sun
And sweet smile of daylight
In my plight I looked at the wondrous cross
Whose Sign is seen in the earth, sky, and sea

With a voice saying "There's hope for the living"
"And two is better than one"
With my last breath I called "JESUS!!!"
The heavens parted with thunder
And then the Dawn came
All eyes saw Him in the sky
It became Daytime forever
And my woes and wretchedness
Was cast into the second death
Paradise is now my home
Where the bonds of brotherhood lives forever and ever
With sweet caresses of righteousness
And melodious music of peace.

AUTHOUR'S NOTE: NONE

(5)   **A PRAYER**

Keep me safe within these walls O LORD
Let not my heart stray from life and reason
May the hunter not find me
For all the years I had known was pain
Filled with hopelessness and hunger
At times I think of padre DD
Whose wish was to know the hunter
And his own white and green fields.
Though he could be right
As his flame of laughter pierces the shadows of cruel nightfall
But my refuge is in You O LORD.
Take not the golden lands from me
Let not my nights be filled with guns and pistols.
Except it be a warning I must heed
Let not my sun go down into the oceans of Atlantic circles
But let my eleventh star stand as a pillar in the brow of heaven
May my faith be kindled by the fire of Your Word
And let not Your altar depart from my heart
May paradise be my home
And Jacob's Pillar Of Stones my resting place
Let my dreams be filled with Angels descending and ascending
And let my last scene be within Your promise and love; resting forever in Your bosom.
Amen!

AUTHOR'S NOTE: NONE

(6) FAMILIAR WAR

You're my brother
But I rather love a stranger
Than embrace you my brother

You're the son of my mummy
But I rather brand you an enemy
Than call you my sibling

By birth we are friends
But I rather see your end
Than hold your truce of amend

For your heart is like the devil
A true blood of evil
Just like the idols

You're no friend of Jerusalem
Neither do you regard the God of Salem
Judgment will come on you like Babylon; The fallen!

AUTHOUR'S NOTES: NONE

(7) FACE TO FACE WITH THE MIND GODDESS

I sat face to face with the Mind goddess
Telling my symptoms and tribulations
Her counsel was more alluring than her business
My past of shame and terrible situations
Was crucified with a confession to the Mind Priestess
Whose doing traced and killed on her altars the evils of my heart's emotions
Her questions like a scanner reading between the lines of my words
I felt polygraphed, yet I never felt such burden lifted from my heart
There was love, care and concern to the end from the very start
I felt reborn not as I was previously born; it was true rebirth
I said so much I never dared I could say
Hopeless was the past, and surer the future as my heart feeling good today
The Mind goddess and Mind Priestess was a helping hand to the mystery I faced
But Jesus Christ is the God of gods and the very One I praised

AUTHOR'S NOTES:

Mind goddess: A metaphor for a psychiatrist

Mind priestess: Psychologist

Crucified: Relieved from pain.

Altars: Notes and therapy.

Rhyme Scheme: ababab cddc, ee ff

(8) THE TRIPLE SIGN

She makes the triple signs on her forehead
Everyday, every night, every now and then.
She does it even when it's cold or red

She bears the T-Mark on her phone
It's on her face, body, clothes, and owns
It's everywhere, even with an altar in her home.

And this mark is a mark of a legion
About their ways, their practice, their religion
It's on her and people of many million

This mark will not see the sun
Nor enter the Light. For it's a mark of a woman and son
There she is, drinking blood in wickedness and having fun.

Judgment has been decreed by the Lamb's Blood!

AUTHOR'S NOTES:

Line 7: It is mingled in political power.
PICTURE:

(9)   HELL IS NO PLACE CALLED HOME

Hell is no place called home
Only an excursion
All the facts you will know
It calls for attention
Don't let it reap your soul
By praise or impression
Nor let it gain control
Who knows its detention
Can be? It dies by fight
And faints by fire and force
Battling by day and night
To win the phrase "It's yours"

Hell's indeed a corruption in deep
Whose decayed tortured can never sleep

AUTHOUR'S NOTES:

(10)　　　**THE CRASH**

I heard Him say to Mrs Belle
"You will score five
On your one seventeenth birthday"
"0 five, 0 six", she replied
But I was silent
Knowing she knew not
What she had said to Gaius Octavius moon
for she was dozing in Lunar Twelve
In the dangerous class room
Before her day of doom

I looked at Mr Soul
And Wished I had much to tell
"That path is crooked to hell
So turn around and save your birds"
Look! (It was a voice)
Man's number is upon you
On the tenth of after Tiberius birth month
Will drink your red inks and burn your robes
To score you five with perfection
In the dangerous oldest month
See rain welling from sorrow hearts
And the Birds nest was accused
O! LORD, rest their souls

AUTHOUR'S NOTES:

Mrs Belle: Bellview airplane
Mr Soul: Sosoliso airplane
5: 2005
117 birthday: 117 passengers that died
0 five 0 six: uncertain for the crash(2005,2006)

Gaius Octavius moon: Month of October
On the tenth after Tiberius Caesar month: 10th of December, Tiberius Caesar was born
in the month of November (16th)

Five with perfection: 2005
In the dangerous oldest month: December (African see the last four months of the year as dangerous, often referred to as the Mber Months)

Birds nest was accused: Blames on the airport management

(11)   **MALARIA AND TYPHOID**

The sun in my head
Crushed me and all my bones
Then the clash of the white razors began
Just after the headache drama upstairs

My window lights coloured yellow in pain
With weight and weakness
My skin was not mine
As I staggered to the bed; my friend for help

But my friend became an enemy
For his philosophy darkened my psychology
As I was been driven endlessly in a terror race
I sought Time, Food, and Grace
But Time became boredom
And Food rejected by my stomach god
And Grace forever delayed

And as my shivers came
It doubled the fever
When dipped in warm baptism-poured
My teeth quivered
As I passed the yellow liquid

And as the god of hunger travelled
With my strength out
His altars could receive no sacrifice
Regardless the number or price

My ghost got caught between Heaven and Hell
As I waited the pending noon
And suffered; troubled, sleeplessly through the evil moon

And as the dawn came;
The sun arose in the middle of the sky
The word was handed over to me
Without ado
In some sort of riddles

By the Drug Duke and his Angels
In his white house of sanctity

"Sir!" He said
Salmonella Typhi
And Plasmodium falciparum seen(+)

		O	H
S. Typhi	D	1:80	1:20
S. Paratyphi A		1:80	1:20
S. Paratyphi B		1:40	1:20
S. Paratyphi C		1:60	1:40

I went back to sleep
As the sanctity bags filtered my blood pipes

AUTHOUR'S NOTES:

Drug Duke: Physician or Pharmacist
Angels: Nurses
White house of sanctity: hospital
Salmonela Typhi and plasmodium are the organisms responsible for malaria and typhoid
Sanctity bags: Drips received during treatment
Blood pipes: Veins
Terror race: Nightmares and dizziness
Time became boredom: Hopeless at the point

(12)   TO MY BROTHER (A SONG)

From the gates
They said goodbye
A common word
Spoken by the men in black
The physician can do no wrong
And the temple messenger sang his songs
A tear and many tears flowing
A bleeding heart has caused the sky
To weep coldly on dirty patches.

On my knees
In supplication
To the Comforter for comfort
Upon the departed
And that the little hairs
Will depart not soon nor
See neither pain nor vanity.

It seems only yesterday
But it was a long time ago
The earth may have covered you
But your names are written in the sun
Written on the moon
Shining like the stars
It is there within the winds
Even the seas resounds the echoes
Of the name Heaven called you

From the middle of the road
We said goodbye
A usual word
Known to the sorrow hearts
Who wondered if it was
The Maker or the Baker?
But we knew you
It seems only a minute
But it was many hours ago

Midnight may have swallowed
A beloved one
But the morning will give
Birth to sons of salvation
And your memory will
Live longer than a thousand hopes

At the last minute
I said goodbye
To my friend
Dressed all in white
Reading the psalms and the poetry
It had only seemed a time
But it was many years ago
I carried you in my heart
As a mine would gold
For yours is a beautiful mind
In it you were braver than a lion
You were swifter than an eagle
Gentler than doves
And wiser than serpents
Why did you ever had to leave?
Many a time I longed
For your kind words
And knightly counsel
Which no mortal can replace!

At the round table;
Before the other knights
All say:
"Why did the earth rob you of your time?"
For you were yet to rule
Before the Eternal called you Home

Now
They, We, I and All say
Well-done!!!
Welcome!!!
Uncommon words to strangers
But only to your nobility
Spoken by the Men in White
It might have seemed a thousand years here
But it was only a day over there.

AUTHOUR'S NOTES:

For Kenneth Chinedu Uduji
They, We, I, and All say "Rest In Peace"

He was more than a brother; He was my friend
I dedicate this poem to you as a token of my love....

(13)   SWEET SORROWFUL SONG

You have every right to let
The mother tree drop her fruits to
Those who ask for it
After all, the gardener had gone on exile
For he himself is not sure when he will return
He was called out by passion
Unprepared he followed
The winding way into the jungle
That he may hang the Monet
On the last wall of his ancestor
And look upon it with pride
So at midnight he steals into the wild;
Across the oceans and farms
His hunger for honor
He quests to kill
And his thirst for dignity he may one day assuage
Like a knight he must prove himself in combat
For that is how a knight's true nature is confirmed

He remembered
"Nobility is not who you are, but what you do"
O my fair lady!
Bruised, though I must be
A minute I spent with you grows to a thousand years

O' Book goddess
If only all the books could read your beauty.
They will find my name in all the pages
But who am I to address a Queen when am not yet a knight?
In the deep, in wild,
In the ocean, in the skies
I searched for you night and day in the night visions
But saddened it was an illusion

Goodbye I say from the valley
Fair well I say from the mountain
You have taken the path ahead the crossroad

And I must walk alone
Please do not look back
Lest you see me cry
For why should a Queen beware of a commoner?
It's not your mosquito; so I must be bitten alone

In the watch of the night:
I could hear the songs of birds
Escorting me on the highway of this lonely odyssey;
A journey I know not when I will return
If only you could hear these songs
Perhaps then you'd see am innocent and convicted of loving you
But guilty and acquitted of loosing you
And so long that yesterday told today of us
So long that today will give birth to tomorrow
I will always think of you.
Goodbye my love!

Authour's Notes: I had to let her go when I heard she broke her promise.

She's the most brilliant woman I have ever met
That is why I called her Book goddess; a metaphor for academic brilliance...

(14) IF ONLY

If only.......

If only you can hear my heart for a moment
If only you can stare once more;
It is beating like the African bongo,
It is darker than midnight.

If only you could see my eyes now
If only you could take a peek;
They are welling with tears,
They are saddened like a lake, like the dew of the Afri-storm

If only you could read between my lines
If only you could listen to my songs;
They are finer than the verses of Shakespeare,
They are sweeter than the melody of Angels.

If only you could permit my promise
If only you can save my oath;
It is Honey from Heaven,
It is paradise forever!

O! Petite!
If only.......

Author's Note:
Do not get me wrong. Not in competition with Shakespeare, just a hyperbolic phrase
to beautify the meaning.

(15)   A PSALM

For those who stand by waters
To invoke signs and wonders
Prophesying confusion
And futility
Those who misled my brother
To serve and sell to hell's leader
Gaining zero and minus vision
In this mortality
To princes on the thrones
Ignoring their father's sons
Leaving them in servitude
To slaves occupying palaces
Forgetting the man who had set them free
For my mother and many children
Those evil songs gotten from
Hell's kitchen
Those who then hated
Each other in ignorance
And the very knowledge haunting
Their shadows and spooks at midnight
And those who refuse to go home
When the sun is awake.

I remember!
The times and lies
The fowl that cares for her eggs
Yet would not let them hatch

I remember!!
The hour of sorrow with voices
In the nerve and bones
Drowsing, sleeplessly, and painfully
Without rest nor relief
And the man who owns the chamber
Had erred to pity

But Grace was approaching him!!!

The chiefs were three,
Addressing the Chief under
The seven suns before the sky
It was in that very night
That the ghost of sorrow left
My bedroom
When the three women
Were sited as I walked in
And my father's eyes were diamond
As he smiled a million dollars to my soul
When in that instant I came back from God
With the news of liberty

The sun, the one, the time then defiled.

The stars assembled in the North
With yam, with its seasons
Remaining ruler, rounding
The sun, ascending in celerity
To his royal throne

Author's Note:
Seven suns: seven days
The Chief: Heaven
The three chiefs: Spirit, soul and body
The sun, the one ,the time then defiled: A new era began, the old abolished
The sun ascending in celerity:
The new man sailing

(16)   **SALVATION**

Christ died on the cross

To save all

Men from Death and loss

Author's Note: John 14:6, Acts 4:12

(17)   CHRIST HANDS RESTORED HER LIFE

The girl is not dead but asleep

She's not in hell, only the deep

Jesus takes her by hand to rise

She sits with wide awakened eyes

New, but news circled that region

Back from the grave; from Death's prison

She's whole, alive from that moment

And far from the land so silent

"Go away! O send them away!"

Send out the crowd; let no flute play

Their disdain had killed the revived

And their songs lends no aid to life

"Jesus! My daughter has just died"

Christ hands on her restored her life

Authour's Note: This poem is a story from the Bible
(Matthew 9:18-26, Mark 5:21-43)

Eight syllable in each of every line

Rhyme scheme: AA, BB, CC, DD, EE, FGFG

(18) MORALS IS A LEARNED MAN

Morals is a learned man
For he's justified by his action
He's a true prince; just like a lamp stand
Beaming the mind's radiation

Moral's robes are never dirty
Nor do his shoes go unpolished
His belt is ever fixed tightly
And his heart forever nourished

Morals is a great precious jewel
Whose founder should religiously treasure
He's scarcely explored amongst youths
Whose death are endlessly used to lecture

Like a warrior holding his shield and sword
Like a champion running his course
Like a disciple cherishing his cross
Is Morals in trials and courts

O Morals; a fine friend of literacy
Whose relative by blood is discipline
A hero medalled with integrity
With crowns rewarding them at the next line

Authour's Note:

(19)   BEHOLD THAT OLD AND RUGGED CROSS

Behold that holy old and rugged cross

Whose crucified I diligently seek

His blood redeemed my soul from Death and loss

Crowning me glories as I stood in meek

Matthew foretell beatitudes as mine

As the Son of Man came forth from God's breast

Presaging the Old Nick's kingdom's arrest

"Seek ye the kingdom; to add all to thine"

His true riches and love; I claim as mine

Without the word, without His grace, no best

Within this world. With the head, eyes, and chest

Survey now that wondrous cross and define

It's love, beauty and His omnipotence

Which has won us for life to His presence

Authour's Note: abab, cddccddc, ee

(20)   MY HOME

My home is above the hills
Just beneath the mountains
From afar, it's as though the sun lives with us
And as if the heavens touch my roof
The dew reaches us first
And the tempest shares no threat
Along the path before the doors lies the lilies
Between the four walls stood a mighty gate called
       "Ebenezer"
Whose failed rival is "Ichabod"

At the sides of the doorbells scents the
Green herbs and red roses
In the morning like spices
At noon like cinnamon
Then the evening like jasmine
Some wish theirs also smelled like....
The walls are concrete and beautifully baked
       How lovely!
They are painted in white and gold

During winter; the Holy doves comes
The spring shows there's work to do
Autumn brightens the smile of harvest
And summer gets us lingered in celebration

The guards are dressed in white linen
And the gardeners' dresses like snow
Even the maidens are covered in wool
And furniture made of jasper stones

It is my home; indeed a home
I praise Heaven for my own
Thank you Father for giving me this home
My home; sweet home

AUTHOUR'S NOTE:

Ebenezer means stone of the help of God, coined from (I Samuel 7: 12)

And Ichabod who failed is that the glory will never depart (I Samuel 4: 21)

Holy doves means Angels

(21)　**A LOOK AT THE CORRIDORS OF LIFE**

He took a look at the corridors of life

    And beheld that justice was expensive

    And mercy at great scarcity

The rooms are doomed to destruction

    With walls painted in wickedness

The halls heavy and hellish

    The steps rigid and dangerous

The roads dark and gloomy

    And weather terrible and murderous

He then turned away

Not venturing another day

AUTHOUR'S NOTE:
The poem is for all the stillborn
It's perhaps a or some reasons why they die
Others cry perhaps because it was too late to return

(22)   ANGELS VS DEMONS

The holy doves are two in the sky

I fondly do ask why?

For the fowls are as one in the earth

And most times fly like birds:

    They are never tired

Like compass, the fowls marks circles

Ceaseless, like the watch hour tic tac

Likewise; holy doves are cables

Showing the watcher the next watch

    Until he's retired

AUTHOUR'S NOTE:

Holy doves: Angels (Matthew 3:16)
Watcher: devoted Christian (Matthew 25:13, 26:40-41, Mark 14:34-38)

Fondly: foolishly

Line one and line three: the ratio between Angels and demons Rev: 12:4

(23)   THE SUN

Your terror smokes me, O sun
This your heat
Like a thousand lashes without scars
Though I bled out water
With many painful rashes surrounding me like some midnight ghost

And it is this your presence O sun
Your glorious face
In the midday hour
This your smile
That none can dare behold

I have seen you blink once or twice
As that brunette brow subdued your face
But sun, you did conquer by pace

Your eyes, I have seen shadowed
As your brow weeping a million tears
With your stare looking pale and sad O sun

I have seen your blindness
And pain as darkness
When as Time hurled fluorescent sickle at your sight

Your wonder is indeed exceeding!
And sureness dictates your glory, O sun
That all things on earth is hidden not from your shine
Unless as you turn away
and turn face another day
To uncover the mysteries of the night flies

AUTHOUR'S NOTE:

Time hurled fluorescent at your sight: The moon eclipsing the sun witnessed in 2006
March

Night flies: dark agents and occurrences not witnessed by the sun

(24)   **BIRDS OF PREY**

Compare between these and distinguish
The owl and the eagle with English;
The eagles by days
And the owl by nights

Both birds are of great strength
Their wings of greater length
The eagle preys
While the owl freights

Which between is more deadly?
Which within is most lovely?
A voice like the flute
An eye like a newt

Consider their nesting height
Easy lights the puzzled sight
The owl's flight with the songs they sigh
The eagle's wings, ways in the sky

AUTHOUR'S NOTE:
Rhyme Scheme: AABC, DDBC, EEFF, GGHH

In each stanza, the first line has the same syllable count with the second. Likewise the
third with the fourth

(25)   MY EPISTLE TO THE FAIR LADY

My words are but a shadow
Of the gratitude I would have shown you
If only you had danced to the music I played
Such a fine song;
Written by Heaven
Composed by Angels
Performed by nature
Adored by kings
Envied by darkness,
The stars shine at it
The moon's in love with it
The trees creaking at its melody
And the sun jealous of its glory,
I tell of the zenith of a hundred mountain's peak
I talk of a thousand mines of gold
I speak of a million years of paradise
I pronounce of a ceaseless season of love
I remind of my heart captivated by your smile
And my soul set free from your prison of rejection
Now, Lo and behold only a time stands in the sands of time
And time is no friend of our mesh
For tomorrow I take path ahead the crossroads!

AUTHOUR'S NOTE: NONE

(26)   ECCLESIASTES

I can never dine with the devil
Neither can I embrace the angel unknown
For sadness is not good
Neither is strange honey any better
I detest darkness to the brim
But neither do I favor the red candles
I can never look the man called sun in the face
But the woman moon is too feeble for my adventures
Call me a chicken
Call me a weakling
But Moses disagrees with such

With hatred, do I despise nightfall
Neither do I hold love for the midday sun
The heights are quite scary even with flowers
But the pits are no better even with lilies
Life has but a dungeon of bitterness
But the grave is no venue of delight
Heaven is a crown not easily awarded
But Hades is a medal not easily avoided
Call me a fool
Call me a stool
But by Heaven I testify much

AUTHOUR'S NOTE:
Moses means the Bible coined from the scriptures Luke 16: 29

(27)   **THIS EARTH IS A BATTLE FIELD**

This earth is some battle field
So, then I ask "do you know?"
That sword must be carried with shield
Till a call is placed on your soul
The years are still young
That's why I shall count
To lay forth my true account
Alas! With my glorious song
"As no one is discharged in times of war"
So I had overcome the Old Nick's score
Hath not my testimony a supersede;
Have I not been scorched by heaven's lamp?
Say no more! For my light can't be damp
Anymore. For through the Gate I now succeed

AUTHOUR'S NOTE:

Rhyme scheme abab, cddc, ee, fggf

(28)   DATE ON THE WAY

"Hello!"
"Hi!" She said, staring at me
Stank and wet on my wrinkles
Then she smiled the grin sensing my fright
"How do you do"
"Am-am-am- al-al-al-alright"
My stuttering seemed forever
"How's work?" Something
I had averted to the depth, yet now
Being served on my table before me
She waited, expecting my response
My eyes narrowed her legs; ignoring her question
Gazing her tits and frame
"Magnificent" my heart cried
Thirsty; my thirst littered beyond before
Her eyes now catching my archer sight
"What are you staring at?"
With her head on her fingers, waiting
For my next words, seeing my silence
To be cowardice
My heart pounded "what am I to say?"
A heavy sigh, and then came a little courage
My eyes to hers, then she came again:
"What exactly do you want-"
At a clash we came together
"Ah-em" - "from me?"
"Tell me exactly?"
"My heart blows like a red joint double sickle-like balloon
Whenever you pass" I spat before a second
And continued;
"And its fever shivers my brains and veins to pity"
"Am I ma-maki-making sense?"

My brows strayed from hers........Idiocy
Silent, silence continued
Only the rhythm of my breath
And the echoes of my heart drum

Remained. Her gaze, zoomed on me
Guiltily; I saw the ghostly No
"It's either win or lose" I muttered to myself
Then, I looked into her eyes
Now, idyllic. Her crescent broadened
As she said "I see no Pinocchio in your face

AUTHOUR'S NOTE:
Pinocchio means lies, untrue, dishonest, or something not real

(29)   HAIL TO THE HERO

Listen to my story..........

The sun woke up the earth in the morning
And slept perpetually in the evening;
Even it was a cold and dry midday
I engaged in thanks and the psalmist way

I remember the youth of the fair moon
When her love burned hot with the sun as noon;
And the stars shining in sight as the sun
Shining gorgeously till the break of dawn

News that the sun has slept eternally
Unexpected truth but eventually;
His dreams were the visions of tomorrow
For our Heavenly Gold has cured sorrow

Now at the bold and bright yam Duke's funeral
There were no rains from dull eyes nor sad minstrel;
Just some wolves in sheep clothing and angry shots from their riffle
And the temple messenger saying his songs and oracle

The sun was truly a hero of his earth
That kings came to the opposite of his birth;
Seeing futures giving us medals and pronounced
Me a prophesy professor as ere announced

I give God the glory......

AUTHOUR'S NOTE:

Sun: father
Moon: mother
Stars: siblings

(30) **MY HEART WITHIN YOUR HEAVEN**

My heart within Your heavens
   Bathed my mind in amazement
   For paradise is You
If Your name be Light
   Then my heart was lit
   By Your strengthened sight
And I was veiled by Your Zillion suns
   Blinded by Your priestly power
   Placed bliss and kiss upon my soul
Everlasting! Everlasting! All my goals
   My heart, Your heat; anointed my head
   My ghostly skin painted in purple and red
And my name written in Your Book
   Did not know you are God
   Till was brought back by dawn

AUTHOUR'S NOTE: NONE

(31)   **THE TRANSITION**

As darkness and deep sleep fell on me
The truths of my past scans deeply
On me. And the future start
Picturing through my heart
Of glory and grace
Killing disgrace
By Jesus
Blood on
Me

AUTHOUR'S NOTE: NONE

(32)   MIDNIGHT SERIES

The morning went spent with evening
And darkness and deep sleep followed
I find myself freed from the harshness of the midday heat
And storms of unbearable terror
When as your name came from the whistling wind
Through the sun of life: the orator of breath
It was soft, sweet and gentle
Kind, mild, and bright
And brightened my soul
When as I heard "Jane! Jane!! Jane!!!
You were there
And I was here
When I rose up
I was alone
And had been watching from the midnight series

Authour's Note:

(33) THERE WAS ONCE A DREAM

There was once a dream
Which are we
You and me
It walked the rocks
It sailed the seas
Then suddenly came the storms
The triple tempest
That never paid any salute to the cease
Then I prayed;
O my dear
My beautiful black belle
Deny me not your virtue
Nor receive my oath as a common stone
This lingered
As I pondered
And wondered
If this dream would survive
And if dead could revive?
This you and me
Which were we
Now once a dream

Authour's Note: None

(34)   I SAW A CROSS IN THE SUN

I saw a cross in the sun
And yet it was a shadow
Its reflection was dispersed into the sun
If I am constant
I would open the East windows
I'll reject the moon as a symbol
And serpent as tattoos
No tree will remain in the garden
Except the Vine's
I'll reject the woman and her son
And allow no cross nailed to the walls
Then, the counterfeit cross
Will vanish from the sun

Authour's Notes: Pharaoh in the churchyard

(35)   MY TIMELINE EXCHANGE

SHE:
Dawn wrapped the earth
Earth time tickled by
Slowly like a man bent with age
Aging with a slow pace
Consciousness hovered on the brain
"Hey! Your beloved awaits you
Rise Quickly"
Quick was the reaction as the compass pointed
To the right nook, nook and cranny, all around
But no sight of my beloved
Beloved, the Book goddess routes this to you
And requests your convey an akin message

ME:
Sound shakes of disbelief
Eyes gazing in amazement
Stood fixed on the idol of intelligence
Often cherished by many men
Now a sun in the weather that kept men alive
Strictly alive from death of dreams
And rekindling of fires;
An era
A future with images of glory and grace
In the same race and difference in place
Time on my watch was boredom
Occupied with battles of ancient dark dreams of my ancestry
To the path I must follow and the mesh left between life and death
Dear, my mind is grace but your love hath not embraced my wounded heart
In the mingling of purity
Tonight I toast to your greatness and mourn at my absence
The sky is falling
The earth is quaking
The mountains are trembling
And God cracks a whip of anger in the dark mist in a roar
Know that my eyes are pointing towards the hills
But my heart still hopes for Eden;
The place of two becoming one
Remember!!!

Authour's Note:
A possible future with the Book goddess

THE TWEET

I walked through the room of doom
While passed the midst on me darkness zoomed
But hopes were rekindled back to life
As soon as you flashed the grin; your smile
Then I knew for sure
Without ado to four
You're the rarest of rays
In a weather and my world marred with shadows
And before the end of these days
We'll be sign for the living as the rainbow
Then came the tweet
Thank you so much Mag
That's incredibly sweet
That's the greatest honour I've ever had

Authour's Note:
A love Poem

(37) THE SKY IS FALLING

The sky is falling
Over there into the sea
I went higher
And behold, it's upon the land
I went further
And it's behind the mount
I boarded a bird
And saw
The heavens all hanging
And that the sky was falling
In some distant thousand miles
Then my reason
Does is season?
When I'm here
It's over there
When I get there
It's next to a neighbour
And if am over there
Won't get to the savor
So!
I gave up this sky fall search
And unmade myself trouble attached

Authour's Note: Just curiosity
And finally stopped bothering myself about the circumnavigation of the earth
Generally, my point is the world cannot be united to one voice
Do your best and leave the rest.

(38) MY AFRICAN SONG

The African flood bled out a river
But it's neither the Niger nor the Nile
Can bear witness to their dark world and while
The high platinum streams flow black and bitter
Its course is being iced by snowy weather
Though an avalanche had done this to file
Out nature's treasure, be it good or vile
The two furnace talents "gold and silver"
They found. Taking back to Europe Scepters
Whose homes are graven with Afri Diamond
With the black sands taken from Niger place
The sun rose to free the frosted rivers
The stars, the moon; bright, big, and in one bond
Upon the Afri-womb and ugly face

Authour's Note: Italian sonnet
Picture:

(39)   **O EPHRAIM**

How many were my tears
Familiarity was the slogan in those years
The war is no friend
True friends are from the jungle
In the jungle said "you overcame the struggle"
          O Ephraim
O Ephraim
You have seen my sorrows
For you know all my groaning and toil
Many were my misery
My melodious misfortunes
You alone know my pathway
How long the road I journeyed
My tears poured like the springs
My wailing like the cousin streams
          Niger and Nile
Those were visible scenes
In the land of odyssey
Where I could have lingered
For not His Finger

Authour's Note: Life Struggle

GLITTER AND GUTTER

Is life full of trouble?
Some do not know what hunger is
They had not been burned by the sun
Nor drenched by heaven's dew
Unusual it is to find the affluent in gutters
Why? For their legs are but tall
And their necks outstretched
Even their eyes demanding and pitiless
Wealth and riches are never enough
So how then is life full of trouble?
Question and reply said "Only these
Are the ones who knows no fun
In the morning gets no bread or stew
Winter spears neither wares nor slippers
Their houses hath but little strength. For small
Seem their daylight, which is considered fetched
All their evenings and midnight are sleepless
They are the ones whose going are tough.

Authour's Note:
Include Rhyme scheme: ABCEFGHI, ABCDEFGHI

(41)   THE THEIF IN THE NIGHT

Offer an incense to darken the sun
Light up a sacrifice to cover the moon
But let foundational stars shine
Even so, let the fine linen stars smile
For no power have the main man of doom
Over the children innocent and young
And the cup of conquest quenches their thirst
As nobles, and as kings standing up first
The caprice now calls the end of winter
"No gnash or dew from the eye" says summer
Then take me away to the street clean and bright
O watcher! Seen the thief in the night?

Authour's Note: Sonnet
About the New Jerusalem, Rev 22

(42)   **IN THIS HEART OF MINE**

In this heart of mine once stood a tree
Right there was the setting sun
When my provoked ancestor cried out against my peace
The one restless knight in his juvenile
Refusing to go home from the river bank
The ripples and boils from the brooks
The ancient drums of visiting terror
A heavy heart of dreams and visions
The goddess of goodness from the pistol land is not his bride
I love heaven to the brim without contest nor denial
But who knows me?
This very tides that rise high like a rainbow in the middle of nightfall
I fell, but on my foot
I smile for not breaking a tooth
I breathe for the air is not mute
The quiet storms of loveless hate
And poisons of some coral snakes
Flows through my blood pipes from Judas
My eyes are not the ones welling like rain
But my feeling of the clouds of AM and PM
A lake I turned my back on
And won't look upon even though
Memories are now families on the walls of my heart and head
I've closed my eyes without intentions
Now, I shut them tight to the dead tree
And to no evil forest existence

Authour's Note: Transition from bad memories